RESCUE OF THE STRANDED
WHALES

Kenneth Mallory and Andrea Conley

SIMON AND SCHUSTER BOOKS FOR YOUNG READERS
PUBLISHED BY SIMON & SCHUSTER INC., NEW YORK

IN ASSOCIATION WITH THE NEW ENGLAND AQUARIUM

The authors would like to extend special thanks to Sandi Goldfarb for her wisdom and support; to Greg Early for his patient help in recreating the story; and to all New England Aquarium staff and outside participants who made the rescue, recovery and release possible.

SIMON AND SCHUSTER BOOKS FOR YOUNG READERS
Simon & Schuster Building, Rockefeller Center, 1230 Avenue of the Americas, New York, New York 10020.

Photographs used with permission:
Ben Barnhart: page 4, 11, 13 *top & bottom*, 15 *left & right*, 16, 21; Paul J. Boyle/NEA: 18, 22, 39, 41, 43 *top*, 52 *right*, 54 *top*, 57, 58 *top*, 61 *top & bottom*; Christopher Brown/SIPA Press: 24, 26, 40, 42, 43 *bottom*, 45, 54 *center & bottom*, 55, 58 *bottom left & bottom right*; Andrea Conley/NEA: 47 *top*, 51, 52 *left*; Paul Erickson/NEA: 31 *bottom*; Patricia M. Fiorelli/NEA: 6; Kelsey-Kennard/Photographers, Inc: 8; Scott Kraus/NEA: 48; Kenneth Mallory/NEA: 9, 25; James F. Murphy: 44; Tim Rumage: 59; Dennis Stierer: 27, 29, 31 *top*, 33, 36, 47 *bottom*.

Cover: Ben Barnhart
Back cover: Christopher Brown/SIPA Press

Designed by Sylvia Frezzolini
Drawing page 12 by John Quinn
Manufactured in the United States of America

10 9 8 7 6 5 4 3 2 1

Library of Congress Cataloging-in-Publication Data
Mallory, Kenneth.   Rescue of the stranded whales.
Summary: Describes the rescue, rehabilitation, and successful release of three young pilot whales that were stranded on a Cape Cod beach during the winter of 1986. 1. Whales—Juvenile literature. 2. Wildlife rescue—Juvenile literature. [1. Whales. 2. Wildlife rescue] I. Conley, Andrea. II. Title. QL737.C43M35 1989   639.9'7953   88-26408
ISBN 0-671-67122-7

FOREWORD

Curiosity and the need to answer questions are part of human nature. They are also the driving forces behind scientific inquiry. This book and the events it describes were the result of the curiosity that has inspired many scientists' commitments to understanding the world of water, including mine.

Science need not be mysterious. It takes much of its value from public support and involvement. And it is often as much a matter of patience and persistence as it is of some specialized knowledge or way of thinking. Many of us spend our careers focused on a single subject. Our studies may provide no more than a glimmer of insight into a complicated process or organism. But slowly we create a small window which allows us a better view of life's complexities. The New England Aquarium's successful rescue, rehabilitation, and release of three stranded pilot whale calves was one such window. It was opened because of the dedication of scientists who have studied thousands of marine mammals. And it was something both the public and the scientific community could celebrate with the same sense of excitement.

During my thirty year career in marine science, I have been fortunate to participate in many of the events that led to this success. I observed my first stranding while employed at Marineland in California in 1958. As is often the case, the public reacted first. Marineland was flooded with calls about a single pilot

A child examines the fluke of a stranded pilot whale.

whale seen milling dangerously close to the shore. Despite our efforts to push the whale out to sea, it returned. Not wanting to abandon the whale we took it to Marineland and attempted to treat it, only to watch it die.

Public response to strandings has always amazed me. When we rescued Tag, Notch, and Baby we received daily inquiries about their health. People wanted progress reports on the whales in the wild. Such public support helps make our work easier and more fulfilling.

The rescue of Tag, Notch, and Baby was a humane response to a mass stranding. We did not decide in advance to take whales from the beach to the Aquarium, but we found three whale calves whose only chance for survival was human intervention. Once in our care, the whales' progress was extraordinary. Soon they would have been too large for the Aquarium's holding pool, so we decided to release them. The successful completion of this project taught us about whale transport, behavior, swimming patterns, social structure, and stranding physiology. Through the release, we were able to learn a great deal, and attract public interest, participation and awareness at the same time. That is a rare achievement for science.

Over the years, I have watched stranding research evolve from beachside curiosity to a serious scientific pursuit. The knowledge we have gained about whales over the last twenty years is significant. Tag, Notch, and Baby were but a few of the animals that taught us along the way. It is our hope that the information we gathered on pilot whales can be used by other scientists and institutions to unravel the mystery of strandings, a quest which may take many lifetimes to complete.

John H. Prescott
EXECUTIVE DIRECTOR,
NEW ENGLAND AQUARIUM

Pilot whales stranded in the shallows of First Encounter Beach.

RESCUE

Greg Early picked up the telephone. "Hi, Greg, it's Bob," said the voice at the other end. "We've got trouble."

Greg looked out the window of the Animal Care Center at the New England Aquarium. It was nine o'clock in the morning on December 3, 1986. Wind was driving rain against the glass, and he could barely see the outline of the docks in Boston Harbor. The tides were much higher than usual because of the full moon. From past experience, Greg knew these were all the ingredients for a whale stranding; and when he heard Bob Prescott's voice, he suspected immediately that this was what was going on. Bob was director of the Audubon's Wellfleet Bay Wildlife Sanctuary in Cape Cod, Massachusetts. He was often the first to call when whales and other wild animals appeared to be in trouble.

"We've got some pilot whales down here, Greg, thirty or more. They're at First Encounter Beach in Eastham. Most of them are still milling in the shallows, but I'm worried about the winds and high tide. I've already alerted local volunteers, but I think you should get down here right away."

During Greg's twelve years as the New England Aquarium's associate curator of animal care, he had witnessed more than a dozen mass whale strandings—apparently deliberate beachings by groups of up to a hundred whales or more. In New England,

An aerial view of Cape Cod. The circle shows First Encounter Beach, on the Cape's northern shore.

most strandings take place on Cape Cod Bay beaches. A look at a map suggests one reason why. The Cape Cod peninsula looks like the curve of a giant fishhook. It juts out into the ocean like a large net sweeping the ocean for food. Ships and animals have a long history of running aground there.

When Bob Prescott hung up, Greg immediately telephoned Jeff Boggs, his assistant in the Animal Care Center. Greg would leave for Eastham right away in the Aquarium's smallest van. He would take his "emergency kit," a kind of doctor's bag equipped with needles, syringes, test tubes, and different kinds of medicines. This equipment would allow Greg to take blood samples and determine the condition of the whales. Because Jeff needed more time to prepare the Aquarium's large white truck, he would follow later. Jeff wanted to install a thick foam pad in the back of the truck in case he needed to move a whale. He also had to pack slings, poles and stretchers, and enough equipment for several days' work.

It is about a two-hour ride from Boston to Eastham. Inside the van, there was a faint smell of baby seals and sour milk. Whales aren't the only animals that get lost. Each year hundreds of harbor seal pups become separated from their mothers and get beached. Greg and his staff had a lot of success rescuing seals. They would bring orphans back to the Animal Care Center to nurse them back to health. "If only we could do the same for the whales," thought Greg.

A young harbor seal. Every year, hundreds of orphaned harbor seal pups are rescued by Aquarium staff.

With Greg was Melissa Schank, one of the Aquarium's scuba divers. As they traveled, he tried to prepare her for what she would see. "The last whale stranding was two years ago," said Greg. "Nearly one hundred pilot whales beached not far from where we're going now." Greg told Melissa that scientists still know very little about why whales deliberately beach themselves. "There are lots of good theories," he said, "but so far that's all they are—just educated guesses. Pilot whales travel in groups called "pods," and they seem to follow a leader. Perhaps a leader doesn't realize how shallow the water is while chasing food near the shore. Or a sick whale may cause a pod to become confused, and they panic and run ashore. Whales are really very mysterious creatures. We usually only see them when they're sick or in danger, or at places like the New England Aquarium.

"We may not know why whales strand," Greg continued, "but we are getting to know a lot more about what happens to whales once they're high and dry on the beach. That's probably the hardest thing to face," he said. "Once a whale has been stranded by the tide, it can go into a state of shock from which it's unlikely to recover. Without the support of water, all that body weight presses on the whale's internal organs—its heart, lungs, and blood circulation system. Blood starts to flow more slowly. And what's even worse, a whale's body temperature can swing dangerously high or dangerously low."

It was shortly before noon when the van pulled into the parking lot at First Encounter Beach. Greg wanted to gather as much information as quickly as he could. It was not yet high tide, and they might be able to do something to help the whales that were still in the water before the outgoing tide left them struggling on the beach.

A volunteer tries to prevent this whale from getting too dry by pouring water over it. A stranded whale is also in danger from its own body weight, which presses on its heart, lungs, and other internal organs.

While Greg spoke with Bob Prescott and a group of volunteers from the town of Eastham, Melissa walked down to the beach. Greg had warned her how difficult it might be seeing so many helpless animals. "We'll be a little like medics walking into a disaster zone," Greg had explained. "Bodies will be everywhere, and we'll have to make hard decisions about which whales might survive and which are beyond help."

A large adult whale lay in the sand just two hundred feet from the parking lot. Pilot whales are small compared with their sixty-foot sperm whale cousins. But at fifteen feet and nearly one ton, this one certainly looked large enough to Melissa. Pilot whales are sometimes called "blackfish." The way the rain polished its melon-shaped head shiny black made it clear how pilot

Pilot whale

whales got their name. They are also called "potheads," and the head and face of the whale in front of her reminded Melissa of the big pot turned upside-down she had seen in an exhibit on cooking in colonial New England. The whale's only signs of life were its occasional labored gasps for breath. Sometimes it lurched its tail, or flukes, as if trying to roll over and back toward the sea. But then it would become silent and still again.

Meanwhile, Greg had moved away from the parking lot. He was waiting for Jeff to arrive with the larger truck and for another key member of the Aquarium's animal care staff, its consulting veterinarian, Joe Geraci. But until they arrived, Greg directed volunteers and members of the Eastham community in

Greg Early and a group of volunteers attempt to turn a pilot whale around and push it back into the open ocean.

the task of keeping the whales that were still in the water together and off the beach. Contrary to what Greg had suspected, it appeared that no single whale had led others to strand themselves on the shore. Whales were coming in along a two-mile stretch of the beach. Despite the four- to six-foot waves, herding the scattered individuals back into a group and away from the beach turned out to be a good strategy—good, that is, until noon, when the tide began to fall.

With falling tides, the situation took a turn for the worse. When the whales could no longer be helped into deeper water, Greg turned his attention to those that had come ashore. Though beached whales are in distress, they don't display the signs of discomfort that we can easily recognize in dogs or cats, or humans. To know what was really going on inside the whales, Greg needed to test their blood for signs of infection or poor blood circulation.

As Greg and Melissa went from beached whale to beached whale, they noticed that most of the adult animals were females. "This looks like a pod of mothers and juveniles," suggested Greg. That suspicion seemed to be confirmed when they came upon two small male whales farther down the beach. One was near the inlet to a salt marsh. Someone had named him Baby, because he was the smallest whale around—only eight feet long! Still farther down the beach lay a slightly larger youngster called Notch, because of a nick in his dorsal fin, the fin on the top of his back. "These whales look young enough to be nursing," said Greg. "There's no way to tell where their mothers are, and they won't stand a chance in the wild on their own. They're orphans now. There's only one thing left to do," he said. "If Jeff gets here

Volunteers pour water over the flukes (tail) of stranded whales to keep them cool. The flukes and flippers act as heat exchangers and help the whale maintain a stable body temperature. Water also helps stop the whale's skin from drying out.

Some of the stranded whales were moved to a sheltered saltwater inlet called Salt Pond. It was hoped that they could be released back into the ocean when the weather improved.

soon, we could try to take them back to the Aquarium. We have a 60,000-gallon pool we can use for an emergency like this. It's a long shot, but it's worth a try."

It was as if Greg had said the magic words. No sooner had he mentioned the name Jeff than the Aquarium's truck rolled into the parking lot.

They had a truck, and they had some whales, but there was a lot of soft beach between the two. The Eastham Public Works Commission had the perfect solution. If its front end loader could be used to remove snow, why not use it to move a whale? Notch and Baby were put on stretchers and then carefully lifted by the plow across the beach and into the truck, ready for the 120-mile journey back to the Aquarium.

While Jeff drove the truck, Melissa sat in the back squeezing water over the whales with a giant sponge. Sometimes when a beached whale stays out of the water too long, its skin cracks and dries. The sponge helped cool the animals as well as keep their skin moist. It didn't matter if it was fresh or salt water, just as long as it was cold. Putting ice water on their flippers, tail, and dorsal fin was especially good because those are the places where whales give off most of their heat. "They're just like car radiators," Greg had told Melissa. "They're the key to temperature control." Greg had also told her to feel their flippers to tell if their temperature got too low. When a whale is in distress, its temperature can swing cold or hot.

When the white truck pulled into the lot at the rear of the Aquarium, everyone breathed a sigh of relief. There had been no emergencies during the trip to Boston. Had the whales panicked and thrashed, they could have torn the truck apart.

Jeff had phoned ahead to say he was coming, so the holding pool's filter pumps were all in working order and ready for the new tenants. John Prescott, the Aquarium's executive director, and a small group of staff were on hand to help transfer Notch and Baby to their new temporary home—but not before they drew some more blood from the whales' tails. Blood tests were the best way the biologists could tell what effect the ride had had on the condition of the whales.

With a "one, two, three, heave," first Notch, then Baby were lifted, walked to the edge of the van, and then slid into the water below. "Glad that part's over," said Jeff. "Now, if they just don't sink or swim madly around the pool." Jeff knew from experience that it takes a while for animals to adjust to new surroundings. Both whales were still clearly confused, and Baby did exactly what Jeff had feared. He panicked and began to swim about frantically. Only well-placed staff prevented him from butting into the pools' walls.

Notch, on the other hand, wasn't going to sink or race anywhere. If anything, John Prescott and the animal care staff were concerned that Notch wasn't sinking deep enough. He bobbed high in the water like a giant cork. Two hours of riding out of water in a truck had made his muscles stiff and rigid. Notch exhaled air from his blowhole in loud, irregular bursts. Baby slowed his pace a little, then lurched forward for a glide, stopping motionless in the center of the pool. "At least they're back in the water again," said Jeff, sighing.

The rescued pilot whales at rest in the Aquarium's 60,000-gallon holding pool.

The staff knew the next hours and days would be critical for the whales' survival. John Prescott was no stranger to whale strandings. His special research interest was in whales. From the sounds of Notch's breathing, John suspected that he, at least, had too much fluid in his lungs. But there was nothing anyone could do but wait. Putting a diver into the tank would only scare the whales. Besides, Baby and Notch were busy sending bursts of clicks around the pool—echoing sounds off the walls to take measure of their underwater home. They needed time to adjust to their strange surroundings.

Twenty-four hours had now passed since the first reports of whales milling along First Encounter Beach. On the morning of the second day, Jeff returned there to help Greg care for the remaining stranded animals. Jeff was amazed at how many people had gathered on the beach—the press, more volunteers, and groups of curious onlookers.

To everyone's relief, the Aquarium's consulting veterinarian, Joe Geraci, and his assistant, David St. Aubin, had arrived while Jeff was back in Boston. Dr. Geraci was now standing in front of a large female whale farther down the beach. As the head of the New England Regional Stranding Network, the New England Aquarium was charged with making difficult and sometimes unpopular decisions. In the Aquarium's view, the most humane thing to do if a whale is suffering irreversibly is to put the animal to sleep. As when putting a dog or cat to sleep if there is no hope for its recovery, it is done with a chemical injection.

"But we stayed up with this whale all night," protested one of the volunteers. He had been part of a group that worked in shifts, pouring water and massaging the whale's massive body to keep its blood circulation going. "You must have known it wouldn't survive. Why couldn't you tell us this before?"

"I understand your feelings," Dr. Geraci explained, "but I can only tell you what I see is happening now. Based on the lab tests I've just received, this whale won't recover. I have to use my judgment as a veterinarian to try to stop its suffering."

Similar scenes would occur throughout the first two days of the stranding. The best that Dr. Geraci, Greg, and Jeff could do was to make careful decisions, give the best advice they could, and concentrate on helping possible survivors.

On the morning of the third day, Greg, Dr. Geraci, and Jeff drove to a saltwater inlet called Salt Pond. Two whales had been moved there by members of two groups, one from the Center for Coastal Studies in Provincetown, and the other from Connecticut's Mystic Marinelife Aquarium. The plan was to keep the whales floating in the pond until the weather cleared and they could be released into the sea. The condition of one whale had taken a turn for the worse, and it looked like the whale wouldn't make it. The other, named Tag after a yellow marker attached to his dorsal fin by the group from Mystic, seemed comparatively healthy.

The members of the Stranding Network gathered around to decide what to do next. The two whales in Salt Pond were the only ones left from the pod. Without the group and with the continued bad weather, Greg and Dr. Geraci recommended that Jeff take Tag, the healthier whale, back to Boston in the Aquarium truck. Again, it was their last option. But, after all, Baby and Notch had made the trip successfully. Why not give Tag the same chance?

Two members of the Provincetown Center for Coastal Studies with Tag in Salt Pond. Tag was named for the yellow marker attached to his dorsal fin.

Unlike Notch and Baby before him, Tag was lifted with a specially modified stretcher. It took extra poles and about twenty people to get the whale finally up into the truck. "He looks about the same size as Notch," thought Jeff. "Maybe they're the same age."

"I sure hope Notch and Baby take to their new companion," said Greg. But he wasn't too worried. Pilot whales are social animals that live in huge pods, sometimes of thousands of whales.

RECOVERY

Three days had passed since the beginning of the mass stranding on Cape Cod's First Encounter Beach. Two young pilot whales named Notch and Baby greeted their third companion, Tag, with hardly a blink of an eye. The three whales were far too busy trying to recover their senses to take much notice of each other. For Tag, Notch, and Baby, transfer to the Aquarium pool was the beginning of hope. The same could not be said for the nearly forty other whales. Twenty-five had either died from shock or injuries, or had to be put to sleep. Another eight or so had been tagged and returned to the sea.

At the Aquarium, the animal care staff was now faced with a dilemma. They didn't want to do anything to upset the newly arrived whales. Tag, Notch, and Baby were frightened enough. But they also knew none of the whales would survive if they didn't get liquids soon. That may sound strange for animals that spend their lives in water. But what their bodies needed most was fresh, not more salt, fluids. Whales receive all their fresh water from their food. A whale that doesn't eat may die of thirst as certainly as a person in a desert.

Greg knew one of the best ways to supply the needed liquid

Baby, Tag, and Notch in their new home at the New England Aquarium.

was to feed the whales fish and squid; but in their current state of shock, none of the whales had shown the slightest interest in food. Hand feeding was the only option. The only way to hand feed them was to remove most of the water from the pool to make sure the whales couldn't move. It would be a kind of controlled stranding in the Aquarium's backyard. With most of the water out of the pool, divers would try to tempt the whales with recently thawed frozen fish. "Let's try herring. It works almost every time," suggested Greg.

During their first days in captivity, Baby, Tag, and Notch were fed by hand. Most of the water was removed from the pool to make sure the whales couldn't move while they were being fed.

The whales were fed on a diet of herring and other raw fish. The herrings' gill openings were stuffed with vitamins and medicines.

It was true. After several unsuccessful attempts at getting first Tag's and then Notch's mouths open, the Aquarium's newest animal care patients got the idea and gulped the fish down. Food and water weren't the only benefits. The herrings' gill openings had been stuffed with multivitamins and medicines to fight infection and disease.

Everyone was happy except Baby. Based on his size, Greg guessed the calf was about a year and a half old. Back at First Encounter Beach, he and Dr. Geraci had thought all three of the whales might still be nursing youngsters. That made a lot of sense in Baby's case. The youngest of the three, he had probably never learned to hunt for food on his own.

Greg had another option. Using a long rubber tube, the animal care staff passed food straight to Baby's stomach. This technique

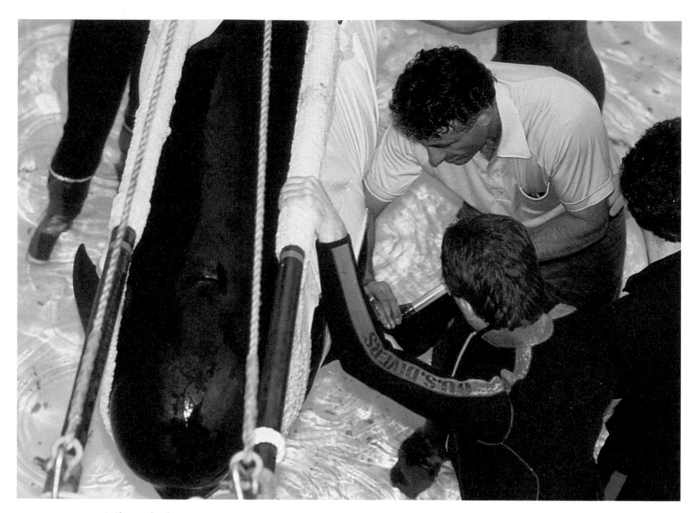

The whales were given regular medical examinations. Here veterinarian Joe Geraci takes blood from a whale's pectoral fin in order to test for signs of infection or stress.

had worked well with harbor seal pups and dolphins, and it proved successful with Baby. Plenty of lubricating jelly of the kind sold in drugstores was used to make the process a little more comfortable.

The way Baby struggled with the long rubber tube, the staff could tell this wasn't the kind of mothering he was used to receiving. "Stay with it," Greg urged. "Baby will relax eventually." Baby did everything he could to resist his tube feeding. He

The regular medical examinations included a weight check. During their six-month stay at the Aquarium, the whales each gained between 150 and 300 pounds.

clenched his teeth and held his breath. He blew salty spray into everyone's faces. He squirmed with his tail. He voiced clicks and gurgles. But slowly, ever so slowly, the continued efforts of the animal care staff began to pay off.

Two weeks passed. By now all three whales had made great progress. They were not only swimming comfortably, but, much to the relief of the staff, they were beginning to accept food thrown into the waters of their behind-the-Aquarium home. Even Baby had come around. A look at the daily logbook showed an increasingly healthy whale:

> DECEMBER 14: Baby stole fish from Notch and Tag.
> Playing with other whales, actively eating.

> DECEMBER 15: Very aggressive, stole a pound of fish
> from Notch and Tag. Ate all the squid offered. Super!

Baby wasn't the only aggressive whale. As the weeks went by, Baby was left far behind in Notch's and Tag's wake, especially Tag's. Although Notch was slightly bigger, Tag soon became the terror of the pool at feeding time. Logbook entries read like police reports:

> FEBRUARY 16: Hungry and aggressive—chased Notch a lot.

> FEBRUARY 17: Ravenous! Extremely aggressive—
> intimidating everyone, eating their fish.
> The intimidator! No one will eat if he is near.

Tag's bullying was a difficult problem with which to deal. From the beginning of the whales' stay in captivity, the Aquarium's plan was to minimize human contact. "These are wild ani-

As their health improved, the whales became more active. Bunched in a tight group of three, they would speed around the pool.

mals," John Prescott said, "and if we ever hope to release them, we don't want them to forget they are wild. If they become used to humans and dependent on them, it may hurt their chances for survival on their own." This policy meant that food was thrown into the water so the whales could discover it as they would in the ocean, not at a feeding station. It also meant that a bully would get the bulk of the food if he wasn't isolated or distracted from his poolmates.

Despite the pushing and shoving at feeding time, Baby, Notch, and Tag had become much more closely attached to one another by now. They certainly chased each other to steal food. But they were also playmates. They argued over fish, but they toyed with them, as well. Bunched in a tight pod of three, Tag, Notch, and Baby would speed around together in their outdoor water home. Sometimes they would bounce or push the fish with the tips of their heads. At other times, they'd swim upside down, playfully lolling at the surface or at the bottom of the pool. One of their favorite games was hide-and-seek. They'd stick their heads straight out of the water to see if anyone was around. Then they'd sink and swim away. Whalers used to call the behavior "spy hopping" because whales bobbed to the surface like a periscope to spy on the outside world.

The three young pilot whales had now been at the Aquarium for over three months. From the beginning of the whales' stay, John Prescott and his staff knew they would face some difficult

TOP: *Baby, Tag, and Notch played at "spy hopping"—sticking their heads out of the water to see if anybody was around, then sinking and swimming away.* BOTTOM: *Baby, Tag, and Notch seen from underwater.*

questions should Tag, Notch, and Baby's condition continue to improve. A release into the wild was a potentially risky option. The three whales could have done well in captivity, but the scientific world would learn a great deal from a successful release. And if successful, Tag, Notch, and Baby would be free in their natural home. Still, the possibility of a release depended on many factors, and foremost was the continued health of the whales.

Fortunately, signs of the whales' improving condition were increasing every day. None was more intriguing than the story of the broken pump. For several days running, maintenance supervisor Jimmy Carr discovered the whale pool's filtration pump mysteriously turned off. He checked everything he could think of. Then one morning he caught the culprit in the act. There was Tag hovering suspiciously near the outlet where the water flows into the tank. "Well, I'll be. Will you look at that," Jimmy said as he watched Tag press his melon-shaped head flat against the side of the pool. "Tag's the one who's shutting off the pump." Tag's pressure against the outflow pipe was fooling the filter system into thinking the water was too low. When that happens, the pump shuts off automatically. "Maybe he likes the sound of turning it off and on," marveled Jimmy.

By now Tag, Notch, and Baby were celebrities throughout the country. They even had their own page in *Newsweek* magazine. Celebrity status was not exactly what they needed, however. As the months went by and John Prescott became increasingly hopeful of a possible release, it became even more important that Tag, Notch, and Baby remain isolated from the

Baby, Tag, and Notch at rest.

public, and even the Aquarium staff. The closest that Aquarium visitors could get to the whales was to watch them through a glass window from the main building. Tag, Notch, and Baby could not see that far, but every day thousands of children waved a greeting as they passed through the Aquarium.

After five months the three whales had each gained between 150 and 300 pounds. They were playful and active, and they swam together as a group. That would be critical if they were to survive in the wild. Pilot whales trap food together in groups. They also huddle in groups to defend against predators such as sharks.

The time had come to decide what to do next. Kathy Krieger, the Aquarium's new curator of marine mammals, veterinarian Joe Geraci, Aquarium Director John Prescott, Greg Early, and a large support staff gathered one Thursday in April to begin the process of planning a release.

Curator of Fishes John Dayton took one of the first major steps. Of all the Aquarium staff, John was most familiar with oceangoing research vessels. John's task was to find a local ship big enough and willing enough to carry three 1,000-pound whales back to their ocean home. Kathy Krieger meanwhile set about the task of designing the transportation slings, boxes, and other release equipment.

Everywhere Aquarium staff went, they were greeted by eager and enthusiastic people willing to help. It seemed everyone knew the story of Baby, Tag, and Notch. At an awning shop in Wakefield, Massachusetts, dolphin trainer Pat Seward found the heavy vinyl she needed to design the whales' transport slings. The store was in the middle of its rush season for weddings and graduations, but it still made time for the baby whales. Similarly with a local foam company. It supplied truckload upon truckload of foam padding several inches thick. Finally, the National Oceanic and Atmospheric Administration welcomed the opportunity to contribute to the cause. It offered the Aquarium the use of its research vessel, *Albatross IV*, docked at Woods Hole, Massachusetts.

A crane is maneuvered into position next to the Aquarium pool in preparation for the release.

RELEASE

Greg Early spent Sunday, June 28, preparing the release of Tag, Notch, and Baby back into the wild. He and his co-workers had been working toward this day for seven months. Now they busied themselves with last-minute details. While the group tested the transport slings one last time, Jeff Boggs finished packing medical supplies and instruments, scuba gear, and rain-wear neatly into large canvas bags. Medical supplies would help in case the whales got sick. The divers would need scuba gear to rescue the whales if something went wrong with the release. And the bright-yellow rainwear would be protection against the rough and rocky swells of the Atlantic Ocean.

The gear was ready now. Still, everyone had to wait for John Prescott to make the most important decision of all: where to release the whales. Pilot whales are social animals, and finding a pod was essential for a successful release, although no one could be sure if a pod of pilot whales would allow strange whales to join its group. Locating a pod might also assure the presence of food nearby. John also knew he had to find a group of whales close to Boston. Keeping the whales out of water too long might endanger their health.

For the first time in the last few weeks, Greg had time to re-flect on what was about to happen. If the release went smoothly, they would make history. Never before had a group of small whales been rescued from a stranding, rehabilitated, and returned safely into the wild. If it didn't go smoothly, if something went wrong... This thought passed through Greg's mind over and over. There were so many things that could go wrong: bad weather; no other pilot whales; Tag, Notch, or Baby possibly getting sick or hurt. But Greg reminded himself that these were risks worth taking. "We're doing the right thing," he thought. "These are healthy whales. Even though they might do well in an aquarium, if we do this right, they will tell us so much more about the behavior of whales in the wild. We have to try."

At 3:45 that afternoon, John Prescott was still trying to locate a pod of pilot whales close to port. Earlier in the day, Aquarium researcher Scott Kraus had flown over pilot whales in the Georges Bank area about ninety miles to the south, but John had also heard reports of a pod just north of Boston. "It would be a lot easier on the whales, not to mention the Aquarium staff, if we could take the shortest route," he said.

Thirty long minutes passed before John's radio telephone crackled to life. "*Shirley Temple* to the Aquarium.... This is the *Shirley Temple* to the Aquarium.... Come in, please" came the voice from out in the ocean. "Sighting of pilot whales negative, repeat negative.... Those were dolphins, not potheads" boomed the voice.

John knew he could wait no longer. "Okay. It's clear now. We're going south. We'll release the whales south of Cape Cod, off Georges Bank," he told the waiting team. "We know Scott saw pilot whales there this morning."

John knew they would need the remaining daylight to move

the whales a mile across the city. There, the *Albatross IV* was docked, its crew waiting for an update. John held the walkie-talkie to his mouth and gave Captain Arbusto on *Albatross* the word. "We're just starting to load the whales now," he said. "We'll let you know we're leaving for the ship as soon as they are settled in the truck."

John then telephoned the Animal Care Center. "Let's move some whales," he told Greg.

"I hoped you'd say that," replied Greg. He hung up the phone, then climbed into the whale holding pool to join the rest of the crew, now dressed in wet suits. The water had been drained to just below knee level, so with a little cooperation from the whales, the divers could move them. Greg knew from first-

The 180-foot Albatross IV *at Boston's Commonwealth Fish Pier, waiting for Baby, Tag, and Notch's arrival.*

hand experience that if a half-ton whale didn't want to move, it didn't have to. Four years earlier, Gred had had an encounter with a stranded whale that he would not forget: One powerful tail slap to his knee and Greg was on crutches for the next couple of months. Now he took no chances.

Carefully, Greg led the group over to Baby. "We'll use the same procedure we've been using for the monthly medical exams," he instructed. It was like roundup time in the Wild West. As the rubber-suited "cowhands" tried to corral Baby away from the rest, the whale whistled a loud protest. Huddled between his older, larger poolmates, Baby did his best to hide from his pursuers. But Greg and the others knew all Baby's tricks by now, so it wasn't long before they had guided him into his stretcher.

ABOVE: *Baby tries to avoid being maneuvered onto the stretcher by staying close to his larger poolmates.*

RIGHT: *Tag and Notch wait while Baby is positioned on the stretcher.*

All three stretchers were lined with a lamb's wool chamois that would absorb water and prevent the whales' skin from chafing. There were holes for the whales' side, or pectoral, fins, and two more for their eyes. Two rings at the top of each stretcher enabled a crane to lift them out of the pool.

After Greg and Dr. Geraci iced Baby down, the crane gently hoisted him out of the pool and inched its way to the Aquarium's front plaza. A large foam-lined truck waited, its top open. As the

Baby is positioned on the stretcher and gently hoisted out of the pool. Each stretcher was lined with a lamb's wool chamois that was kept moist to prevent the whales' skin from chafing. Holes were made for the whales' eyes and pectoral fins.

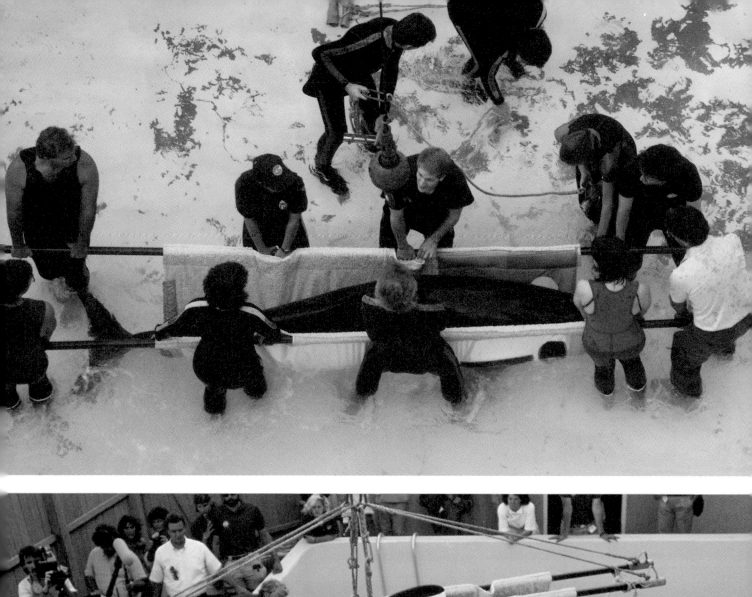

crane lifted Baby up over the vehicle's aluminum side, six staff members guided the whale into his comfortable transport space. "He looks like he's flying," commented an observer. And it was true. With his side flippers hanging down through the openings in the canvas, Baby looked like he had wings.

Thousands of people had come to bid the whales good-bye: news photographers and reporters, children with ice-cream cones, people in T-shirts, grandfathers and grandmothers. A path had been roped off so the cranes could get through the crowds. In the middle of it all, a wedding was in progress on the Aquarium's Harbor Terrace behind the whale pool.

Joe Geraci (in the white shirt) and Greg Early (behind him, in the blue shirt) help clear a path through the spectators as Baby is moved to the truck.

Baby is hoisted into the truck. "He looks like he's flying," said a spectator.

Two long hours passed before Tag and Notch joined Baby in the truck. It took time to assure the comfort and safety of the whales. Though Boston's Commonwealth Fish Pier and the waiting *Albatross* were close-by, two blue-uniformed motorcycle policemen escorted the truck. "Nothing but the best for these whales," thought Greg. No one wanted to risk getting stuck in a Boston traffic jam. Greg, Jeff, Kathy Krieger, and a number of other staff members rode with the whales. John Prescott and several others followed closely behind.

On the rear deck of the *Albatross*, three whale-sized containers stood waiting for their cargo. "Let's speed it up," urged John Prescott. He knew it would be sunset by the time the whales were loaded and all gear was stowed. "We're cutting it pretty tight as it is." John Prescott estimated they had a maximum of thirty-six hours before the whales had to be put either in the ocean or back in the Aquarium pool.

At last *Albatross IV* blasted its horn and pulled away from the dock. The whales rested, cradled in their stretchers, as the ship steamed south toward the famous fishing grounds of Georges Bank. Baby, Notch, and Tag were finally launched on the first leg of their journey home.

The whales were kept wet and cool with sea water. Kathy Krieger had applied zinc oxide to each whale's skin to keep it moist. In the morning, the zinc would serve as a sunscreen, as well. "You guys look like lifeguards at the beach," Kathy said, jokingly. Or circus clowns—anything but whales. But, however silly they looked, Kathy knew it was all for a good purpose.

ABOVE: *One of the whales being moved into his container on the deck of the* Albatross. *White zinc oxide cream was applied to the whales' skin to prevent chaffing.*

LEFT: *One of the whales in his container on the* Albatross. *He has been hosed down, covered with a damp cloth, and covered with ice to keep him cool and comfortable during the voyage.*

The Albatross *steams toward Georges Bank. On the rear deck are the three wooden containers holding the whales.*

A steel maze of research labs, bunk rooms, and hundreds of technical instruments, the *Albatross IV* was designed for scientists who work at sea. In one of the ship's labs, Dr. Geraci and Greg tested blood samples they had just taken from the whales. Elsewhere, Dr. Bruce Mate, a marine biologist and radio tracking expert from Oregon State University, worked to adjust three compact radio tags and a larger satellite tag that would be attached to the whales before they were released. The tags were essential to tell if the whales survived after the release. All three whales would wear radio tags. Whenever they came to the surface to get air, their tags would send strong signals to a special FM radio, which would beep. The loudness and direction of the beeps would help scientists pinpoint their location.

Since Tag was the biggest whale, he also wore the larger satellite transmitter, which would send a radio signal to a satellite that circled the Earth every hour and a half. Scientists hoped it would provide the most information about where the whales went, the temperature of the water, and how often they surfaced or dived.

Although it was nearly 2:00 A.M., there was still plenty of activity on the rear deck. Curator of Fishes John Dayton worked with two Aquarium divers, Dan Laughlin and Mike Kelleher. They were assembling a large floating pen made of plastic plumbing pipes and nylon rope. They jokingly called it "the whale jail," and that's exactly what it looked like. Mike even "served some time" by getting inside to test it. It may have looked like a jail, but its use would be only temporary. When the time came for the release, the pen would be set in the water alongside the *Albatross IV*. All three whales would be lowered into it and then released together. As well as ensuring the whales would be released together, the pen would also allow the travel-weary whales the chance to work out any stiffness before they were left on their own.

The ship pitched and rolled. Below deck the churning seas splashed against the vessel's round portholes. John, Dan, and Mike steadied themselves with the ship's many handrailings as they made their way toward their bunks. "It's like looking through a window of a washing machine," said Dan. Many of the ship's passengers were fighting the motion sickness that often affects seagoers. As usual, Greg was prepared. Georges Bank had a reputation for having high seas, and the last thing he wanted was to feel sick during the release. He brought a large supply of scopolamine, the strongest seasickness medicine available. It comes in a tiny round patch worn just behind the ear. By the end of the night, almost everyone was wearing a patch.

The human passengers weren't the only ones suffering. At about 4:00 A.M., animal trainer Sue Faulkner hurried to Kathy

Krieger's bunk room to wake her. "Come quickly," she said. "Baby's moving. He's restless, and he looks like he's in distress." Kathy sprang out of bed and hurried up on deck. "I'll need help," Kathy told Sue. "Get Manny right away." Manny was the ship's crane operator. "We have to move Baby to the deck, massage him, and try to calm him down."

Manny climbed into the cab of the crane. He then gunned the engine, swung the tall arm of the crane into place above Baby's sling, and lifted the 1,000-pound youngster out of his container. Once Baby had been lowered on deck, an assembled crew slipped him from his sling, massaged him, hosed him down, and gave him a fresh application of zinc oxide. "We should all be so lucky," joked Manny, trying to relieve the tension. Baby seemed to enjoy the attention.

When the sun rose, whale researcher Scott Kraus was already on the lookout for a school of pilot whales. The faint hum of his twin engine plane could just then be heard from the ship's deck. "Whales in sight, whales in sight," cracked his voice over the ship's radio. "It couldn't be better. It's the pod of pilot whales we've been looking for." Scott Kraus then radioed the location to Captain Arbusto at the ship's wheel.

It was a clear day, and in the distance, Captain Arbusto could see the outline of *Yankee Freedom*, a ship chartered especially for TV and newspaper reporters and photographers. Later, the *Yankee Freedom* planned to steam closer to allow its passengers a clear view of the whale release. Until the actual release, however, John Prescott had instructed the boat to keep its distance so it wouldn't disturb the whales.

Meanwhile, Dr. Geraci gave Tag, Notch, and Baby injections

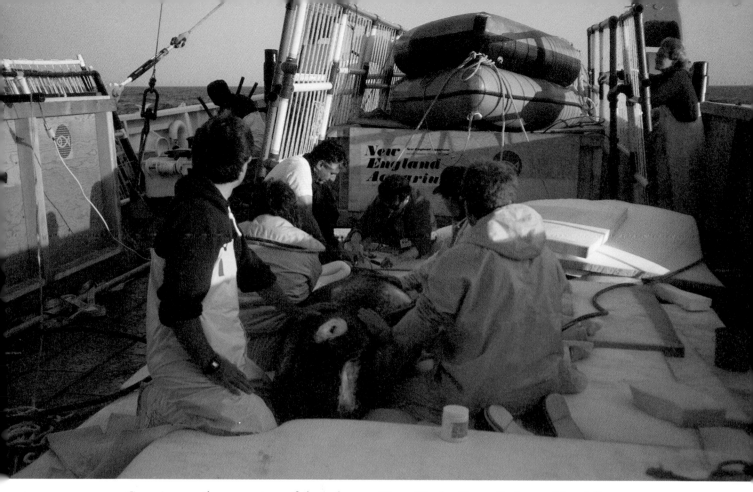

Sunrise on the morning of the release. Greg Early (in red) draws blood from a whale's fluke in order to carry out a final medical check.

that would help them maintain their good health in the wild. He also gave them each a shot of xylocaine, an anaesthetic similar to a dentist's novocaine. Only then did he attach the radio tags and satellite tag to the whales' dorsal fins. The procedure he used was similar to the one used to pierce ears.

"There, off the starboard side, a pod of pilot whales!" John Prescott called, looking to the right of the ship. Whales were everywhere. And they weren't just pilot whales. Humpbacks were jumping halfway out of the water. Fin whales spouted. Small seabirds called shearwaters and storm petrels dodged and darted among the whales, hoping for a share of fish to eat. Tag,

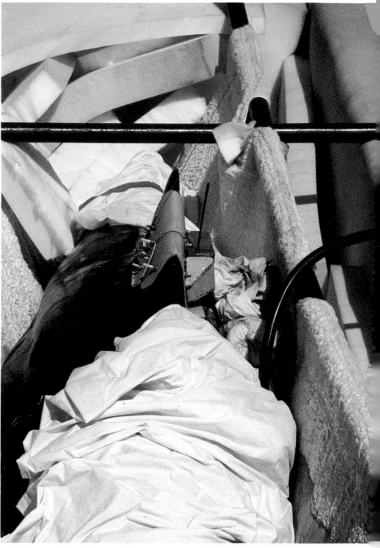

LEFT: *Joe Geraci and Bruce Mate attach the satellite transmitter to Tag's dorsal fin. The procedure was painless.*

RIGHT: *The radio and satellite transmitters in position on Tag's dorsal fin. The silver cylinder on the left is the radio transmitter. The red box on the right contains the satellite transmitter.*

Notch, and Baby couldn't have asked for a more perfect welcome.

Meanwhile, Manny was back in the crane cab again, just hours after Baby's early morning emergency. The crane would be used for a different purpose this time. Manny needed it to set the floating pen, "the whale jail" they had joked about earlier, down into the water by the side of the ship. Three inflatable Zodiac rafts were also launched. They would allow Kathy Krieger, Mike, Dan, and other divers to supervise the release from the water. On the bridge, Captain Arbusto signaled to *Yankee Freedom* that it could come closer. Reporters and photographers waited, pencils poised, cameras ready.

Notch went first. Manny hoisted him out of his container, while John Prescott, Greg, and Dr. Geraci held steering ropes attached to the whale's stretcher. "Hold steady," John Prescott yelled to Manny up in the crane's cab. The wind had been picking up over the last hour or so. The ship was rolling so badly that the scientists had difficulty controlling the swaying, thousand-pound Notch. "Let's start over," John called to Manny. So they lowered the whale back into the container and began again. Slowly, the crane hoisted Notch back off the deck. Again his weight overpowered the struggling crew. This time the ship lurched even harder, and the whale suddenly swung over the side near the floating pen.

"Steady!" yelled John Prescott. All available hands held tightly to the ropes. In a terrifying instant, John realized that if the boat swayed backward, Notch would go crashing into the side of the boat. "Put him down, into the pen, *now!*" he demanded. So down Notch went into the safety of the floating pen, but down

LEFT: *"The whale jail" is lowered into positon. Then Notch is hoisted out of his container, before being lowered over the side of the* Albatross.

ABOVE: *As the ship rolled in the heavy sea, the crew realized that Notch was in danger of slamming into its metal hull. To avoid this, he was dropped quickly into the water, where he became entangled in the pen's rope sides and had to be cut loose. Seconds after these pictures were taken, Notch was free—but not exactly as planned.*

faster than the plan had called for. John Prescott had avoided one difficult situation only to be faced with another. Notch was now too close to the edge of the pen. Without time to sense his surroundings, the struggling whale undertook his own release and plunged straight into the pen's rope sides.

Kathy Krieger lunged over the side of the Zodiac raft and pulled it closer to the pen. "Cut the rope!" she ordered. "Cut that rope" came a chorus from the crew. Tangled in the ropes of the pen, Notch was in danger of drowning. While the Zodiac bobbed in the ocean's swells, first Mike, then Dan dove into the water. Using their dive knives, they cut a hole in the pen's rope sides, allowing Notch just enough room to escape.

Notch was free now—not exactly as planned, but free nonetheless. The only casualty in those desperate moments was Notch's radio tag. Bruce Mate was the first to notice. "It must have come off when he slammed into the ropes," thought Bruce, clearly disappointed about losing one of the tags on which he had worked so hard. Without the radio tag, Notch would be impossible to follow. It was little consolation that Notch's zinc oxide mask made him easy to spot as he swam farther and farther from the ship.

With the floating pen out of action, the team switched to a large wooden platform that had been prepared as an alternative. Known as the "Prescott Whale Launcher" since it was John Prescott's idea, the platform would be like a giant dump truck at sea. The whales would be placed on the platform, which would work like the dump truck's bed. The crane would tilt the platform up, and its cargo would slide into the sea.

Manny and the crane went to work again. This time the hoisting distance was much shorter, and he didn't need to raise the whales as high in the air. Tag and Baby were lowered smoothly into place on the wooden platform. Greg and Kathy slathered the twosome with salad oil to help them slide into the water. Tag's and Baby's sleek black fins shimmered in the sun.

"Okay," John yelled, "you can lift the launcher now." As he had practiced it many times before, Manny raised, then lowered the platform to just above the surface of the sea. Everyone held

Tag and Baby in the whale launcher.

LEFT: *With the whales in position, the launcher is lifted over the stern of the Albatross.*

BELOW: *Once in position above the surface of the water, the launcher is gently tilted, and Tag and Baby slide into the ocean.*

his or her breath. As the platform tilted, Tag and Baby wriggled their tails and slid smoothly back to their ocean home. The crew cheered, embraced, and shook hands. "Two out of three's not bad," thought Greg. Then he saw something off the ship's stern that made him smile. There was Notch, with his unmistakable zinc oxide mask, heading back toward the ship. "True friendship," Greg said, "if I ever saw it."

Baby, Tag, and Notch swimming away from the Albatross *after the release. Tag's satellite transmitter is clearly visible on his dorsal fin.*

But Greg and the rest of the *Albatross* crew didn't say good-bye to Tag, Notch, and Baby on the morning of June 29, 1987. To make sure the whales were feeding and swimming properly, the *Albatross* spent the next two days following beeps from the whales' two remaining radio tags. Fog moved in on the morning of the second day. As the whales played hide-and-seek with the pursuing research vessel, John Prescott and Bruce Mate did their best to pinpoint their location. "I could swear they are only a football-field length away," John said to Dr. Mate. "They must know we're around them. If that fog weren't here, we'd probably see them right in front of the boat."

Loud beeps on a fogbound afternoon were the closest John Prescott and most of the crew would ever get to seeing the whales again—except for Kathy Krieger. A month after the whales' release, Kathy was flying in a Beech Craft airplane specially equipped for aerial surveys. As she flew over Georges Bank, she began to pick up the radio beeps for which she had been listening. By now only one of the radio tags was working, but it was strong enough for Kathy to locate. The day was bright and filled with sunlight. As the radio sounds got louder and louder, she saw a wonderful surprise beneath the plane. Only 500 feet below, two pods of pilot whales were swimming toward one another. And right in the middle of one of the groups was Tag, his unmistakable satellite marker glinting in the sun. Kathy knew Baby must have been there, too. Baby was the only one left with a working radio tag, and it was his signal that had led Kathy to the pod and Tag. "Let's hope Notch is there too," thought Kathy. "After all, he came back for his two companions when they were first released."

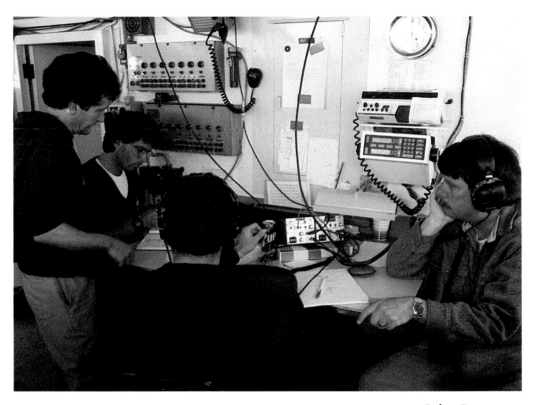

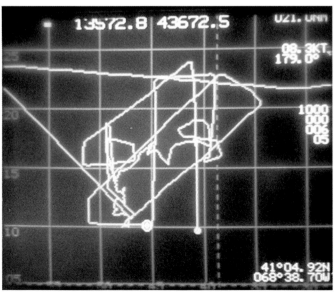

ABOVE: *John Pres-cott (right, with earphones), Greg Early (left), and other members of the crew listen for signals from the whales' radio transmitters.*

LEFT: *A computer screen displays the course of the Alba-tross as it follows the whales.*

From July until October, a satellite in space continued to keep track of Tag's whereabouts. Bruce Mate, the designer of the radio and satellite tags, knew their battery power would run down eventually, and he had designed them so they'd rust and fall off. When the last signal was received, Tag was where everyone was hoping he'd be. Based on the temperature readings from the satellite, Aquarium staff know he was following an underwater

A map showing where Tag went in the months after the release, as indicated by signals from his satellite transmitter.

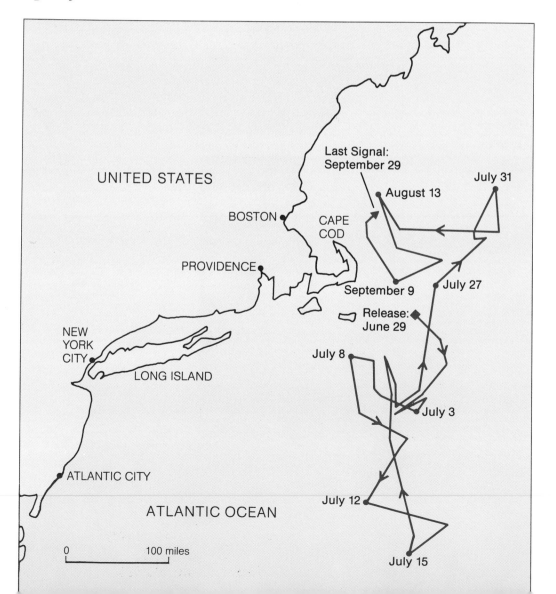

stream of cold water at the edge of the continental shelf, an area where food fishes swim in the hundreds of thousands.

Tag, Notch, and Baby gave us a brief glimpse into a little known world of whales and their life in the sea. We still don't know why whales strand. But we now know a little more about how and where they live. We have seen that, if circumstances are right, stranded whales can be taken from a beach, rehabilitated, and returned to the ocean—and they can survive. We know a little more about how often and how deep pilot whales go daily in search of food. And, although the beeps of their radio tags have long since faded, Tag, Notch, and Baby left something far more lasting behind.

"We gave Baby, Tag, and Notch a wonderful gift," Greg Early said, "their safe return to the sea. But they gave us something as important in return. You remember when we fitted Baby, Tag, and Notch with the radio tags? We saved the small plugs of skin removed when we applied the tags. The skin cells contain 'genetic fingerprints,' maps of genetic information that are unique for each individual whale. If we analyze these 'fingerprints' carefully, some day these small samples of whale skin will tell us a lot about the whales that are stranding on the beaches of Cape Cod. Do they all belong to a family of closely related whales—did Tag and Baby have the same mother or father? Or are the whales all just strangers that happened to be in the wrong place at the wrong time?

"Just think about it," said Greg, looking at the small test tube he held up to the light in front of him. "From such a small gift, a lifetime of understanding."

INDEX